THIS BOOK
BELONGS TO

____

____

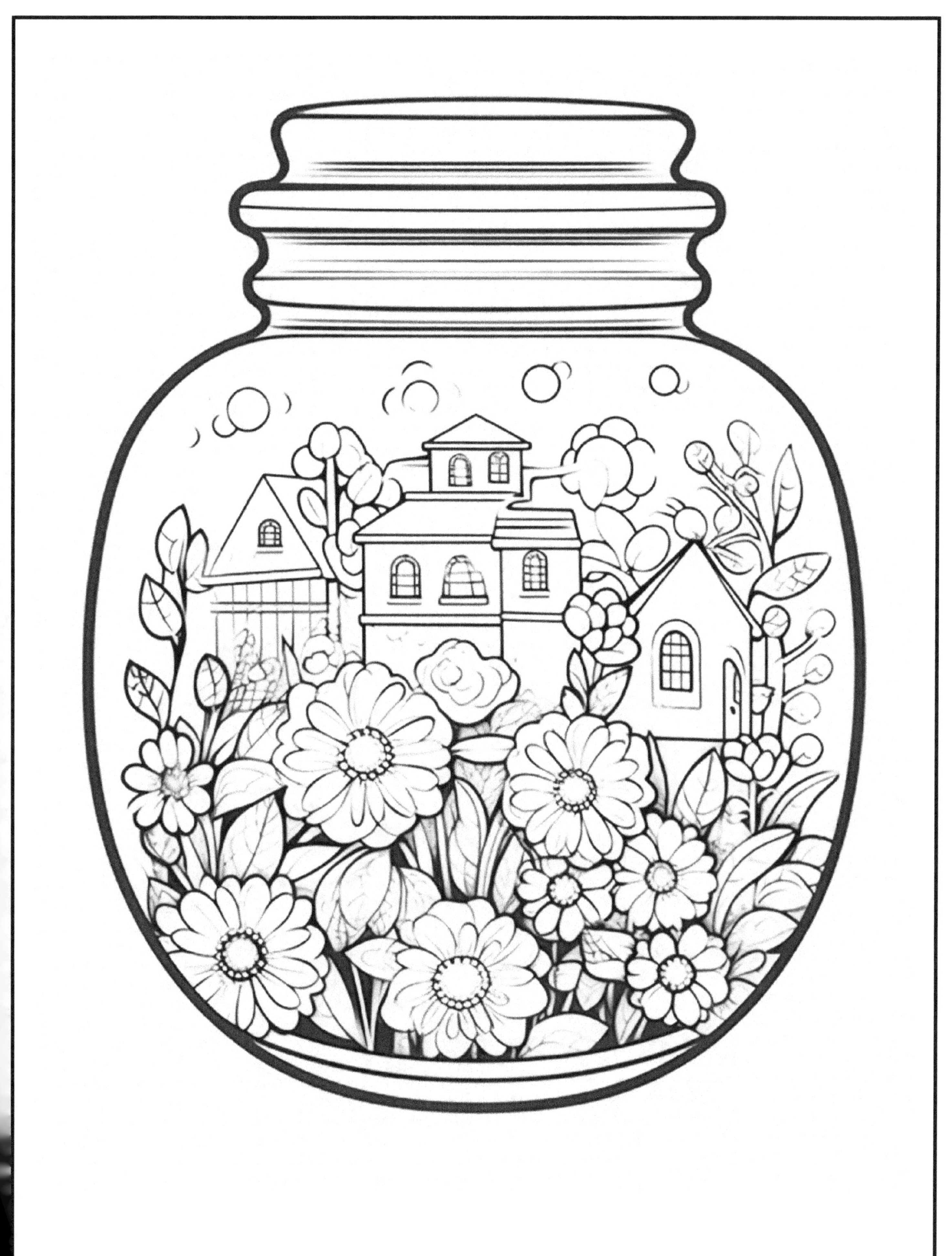

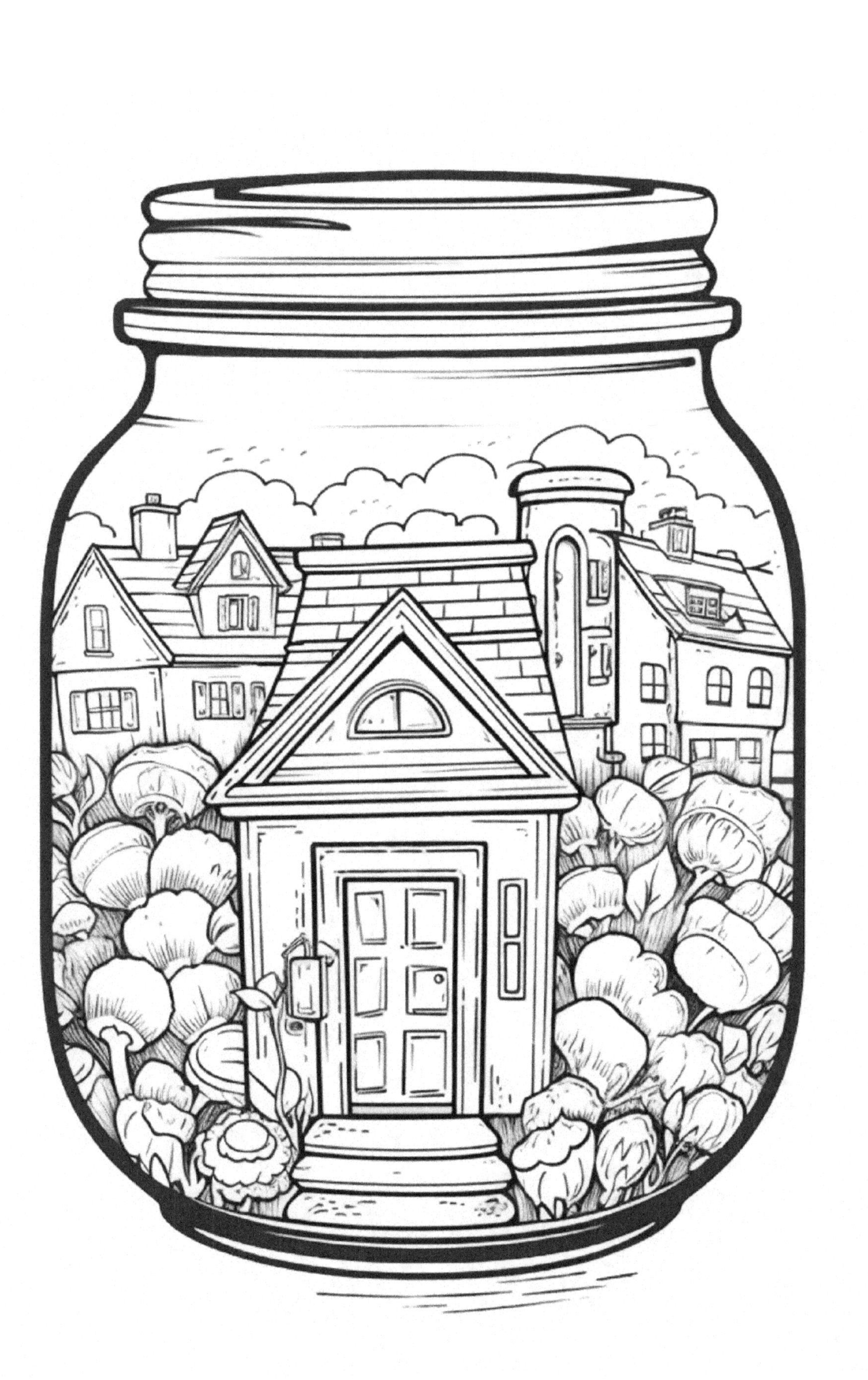

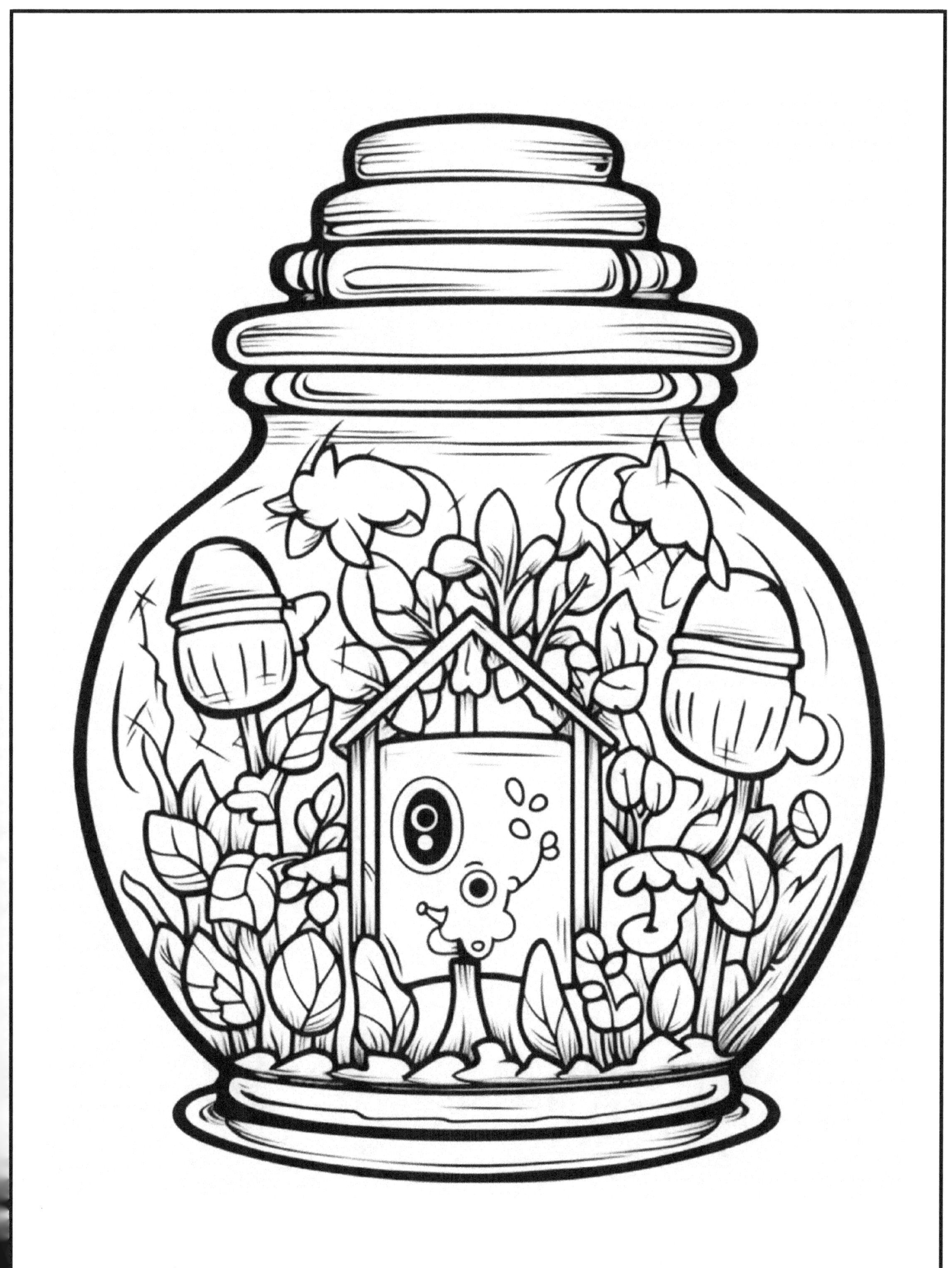

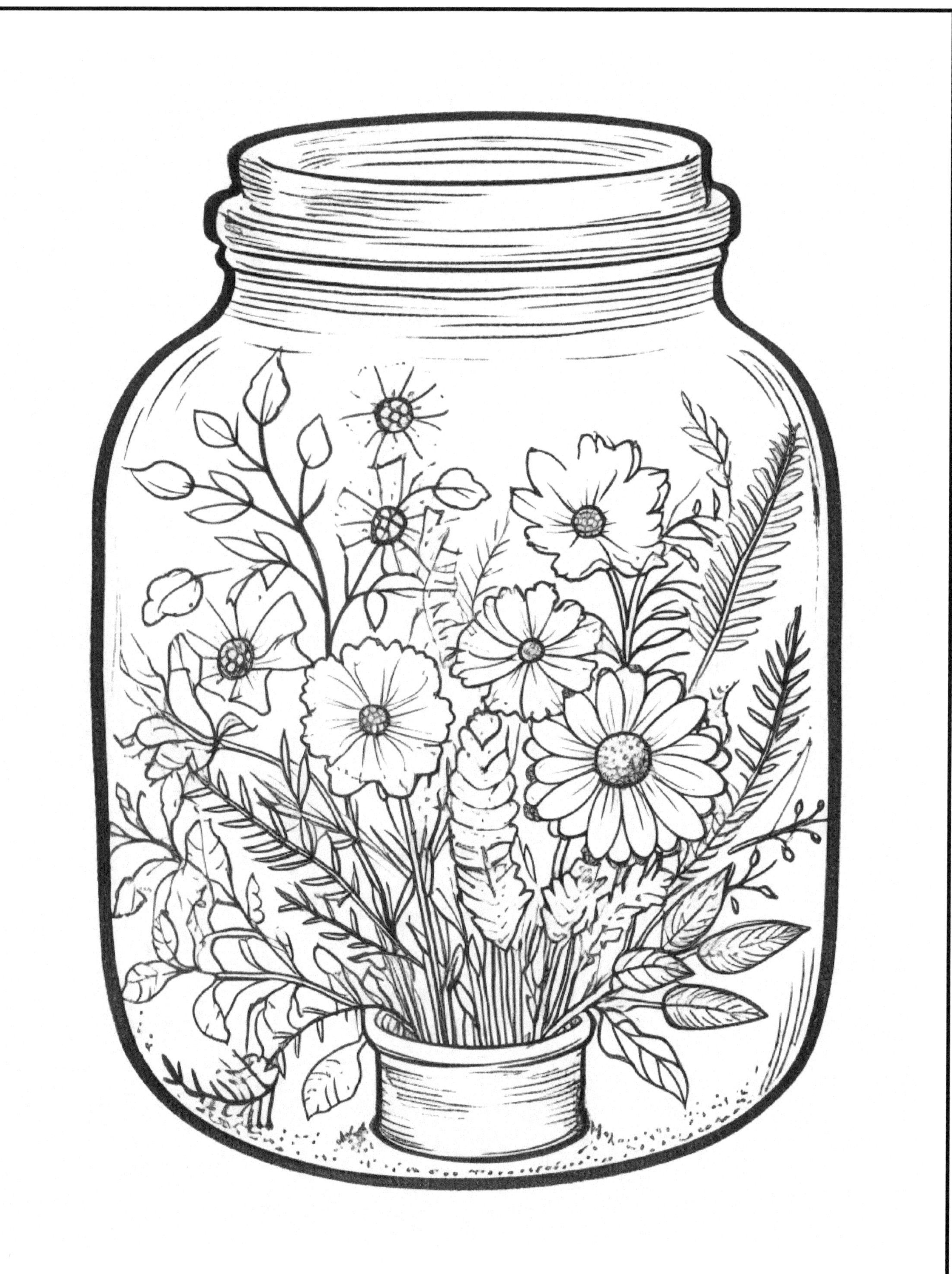

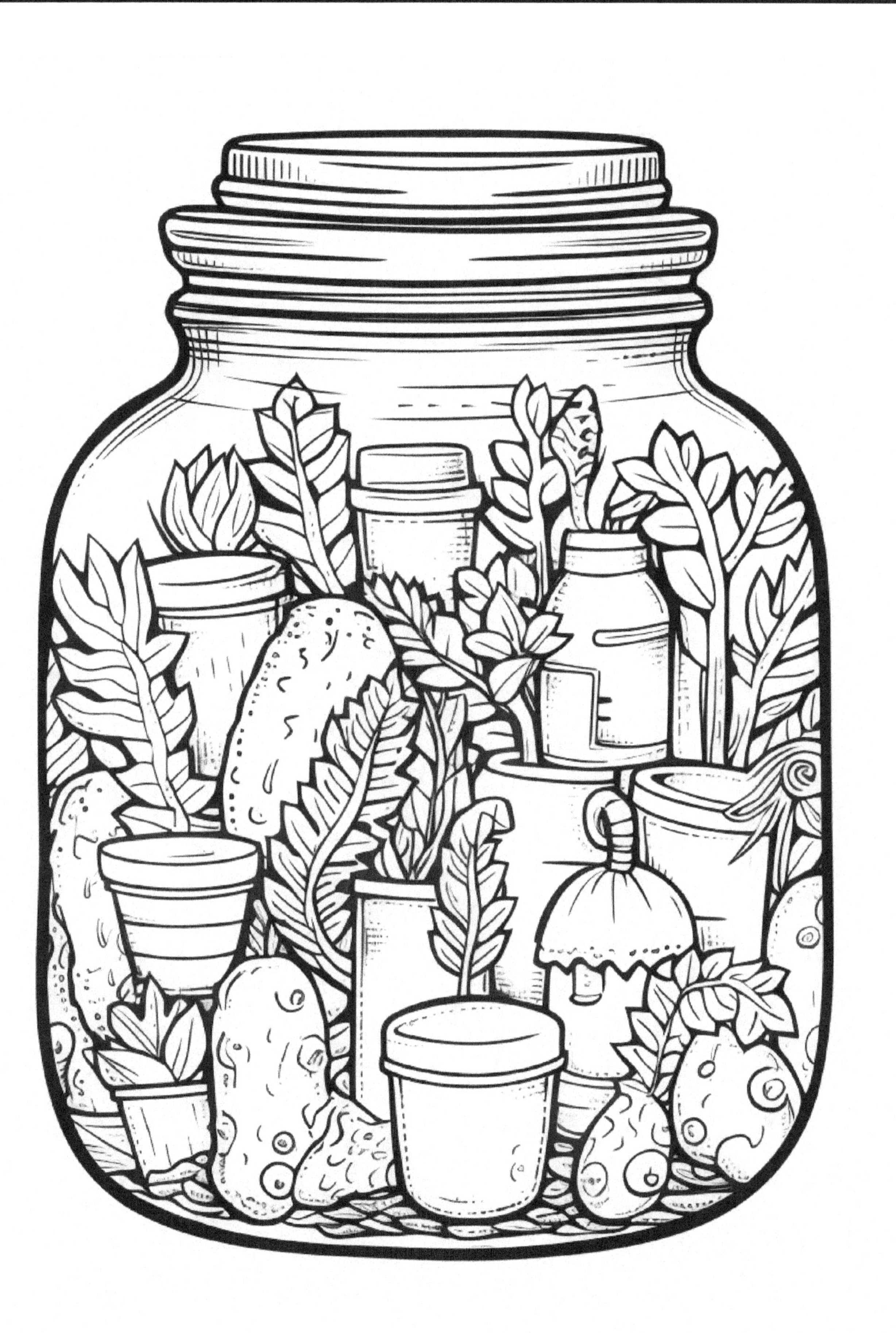

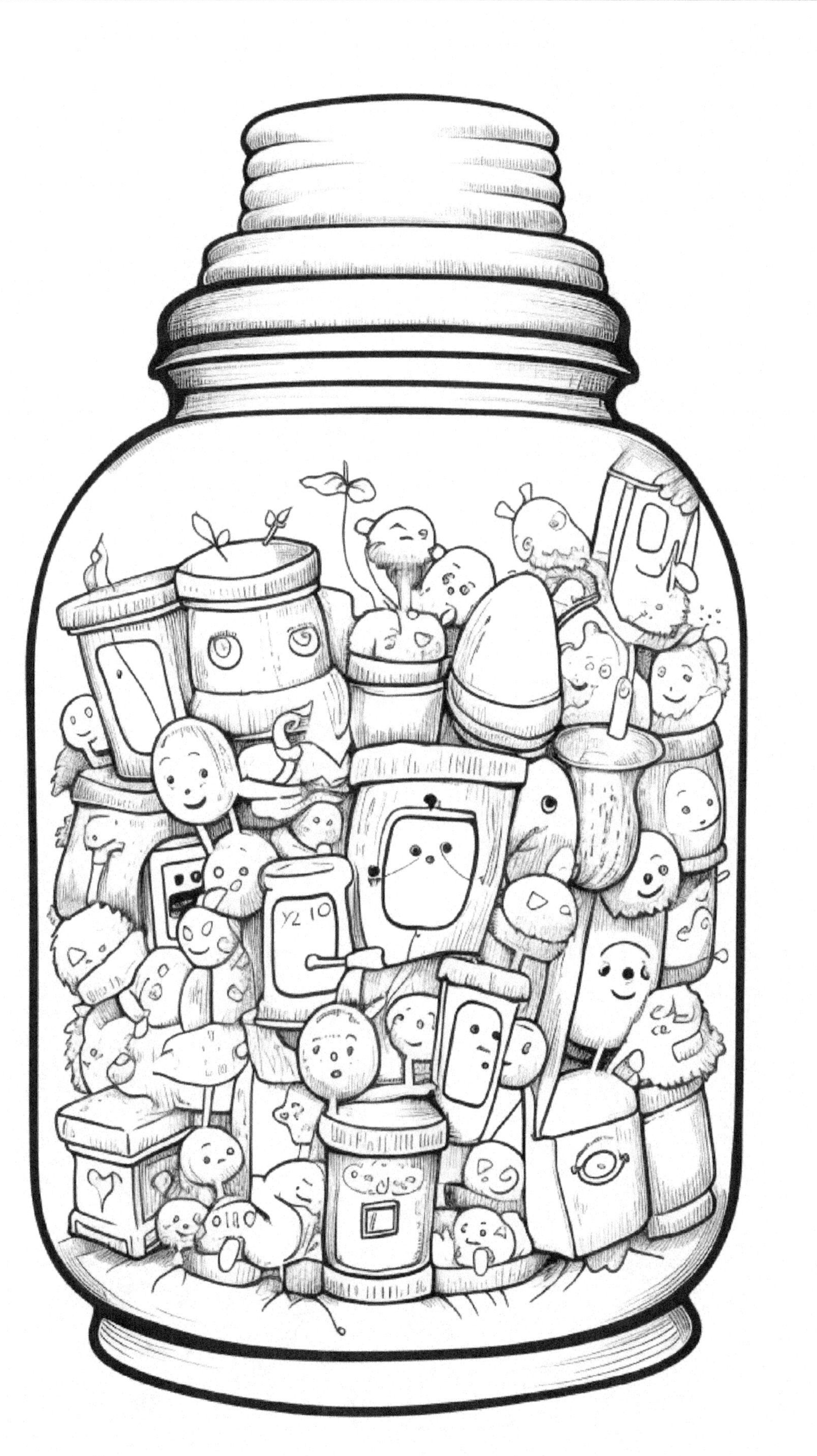

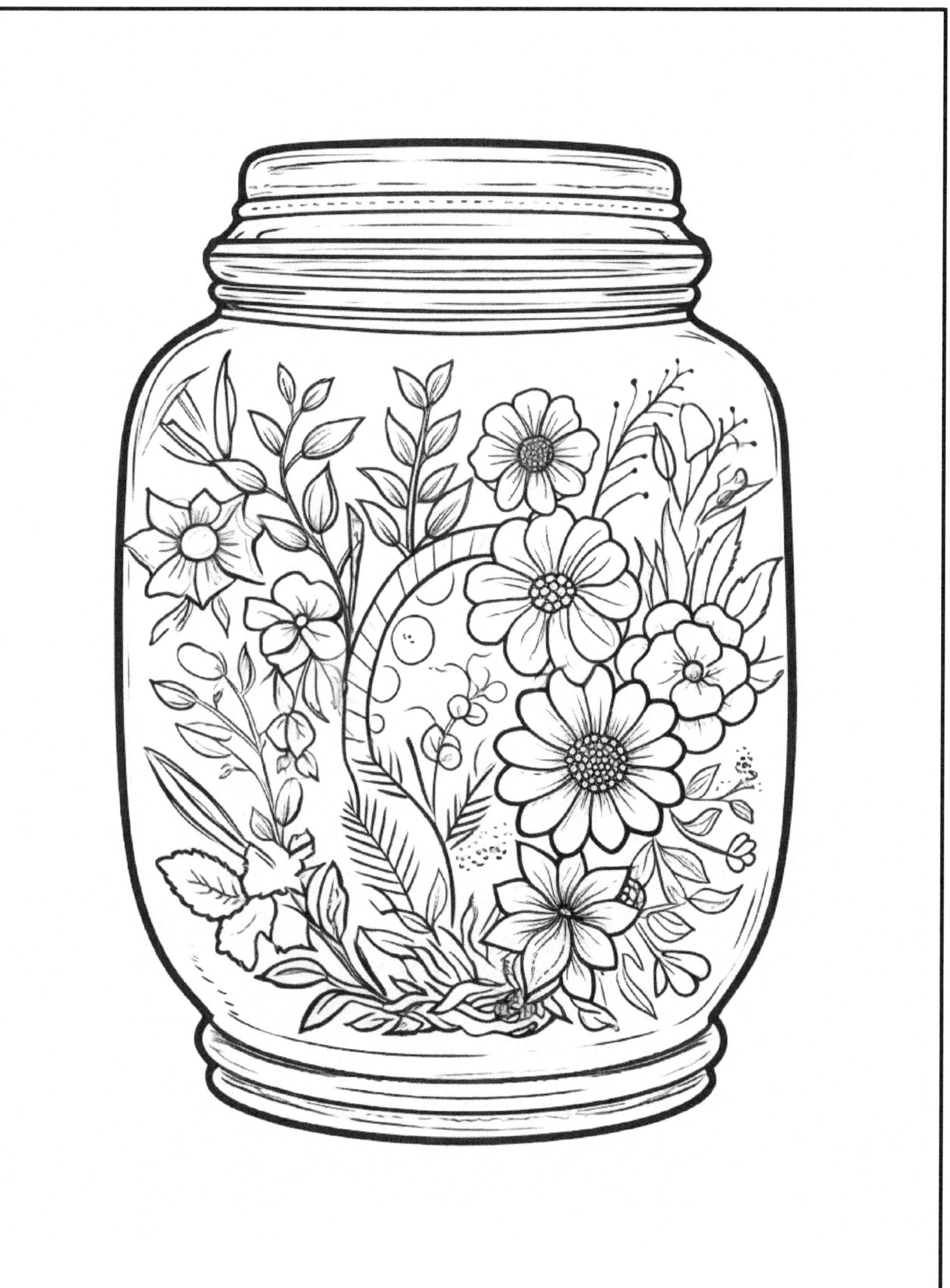

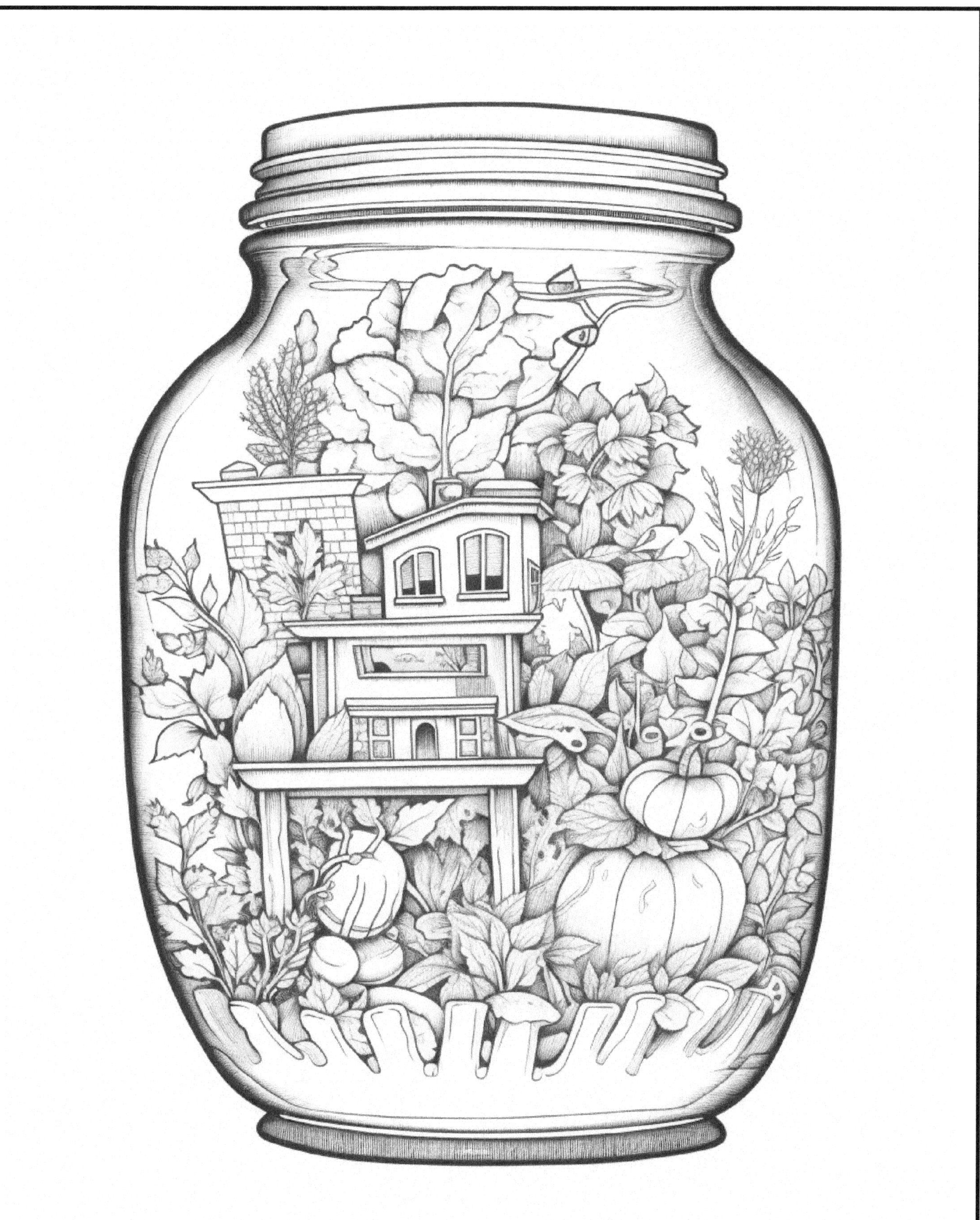

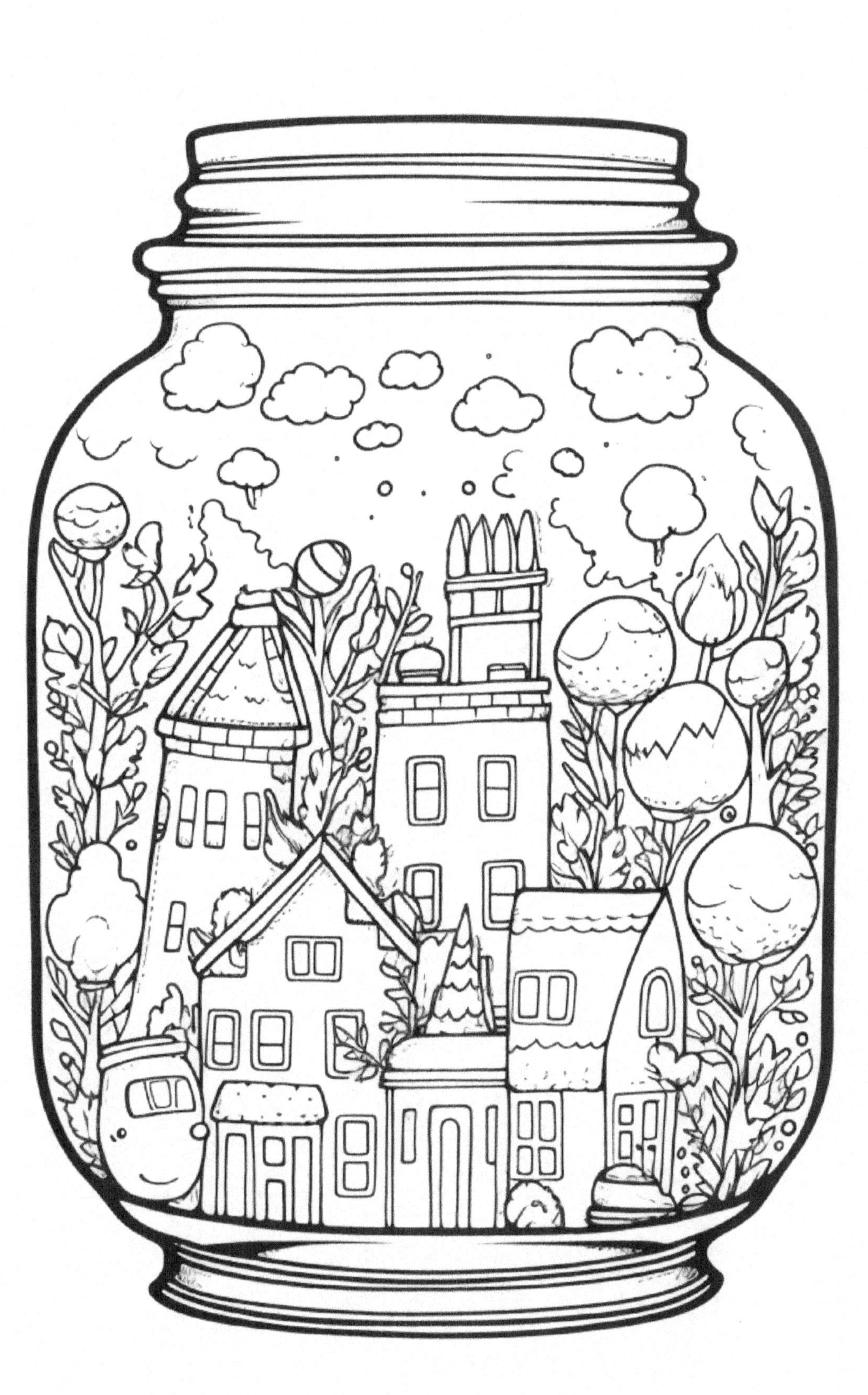

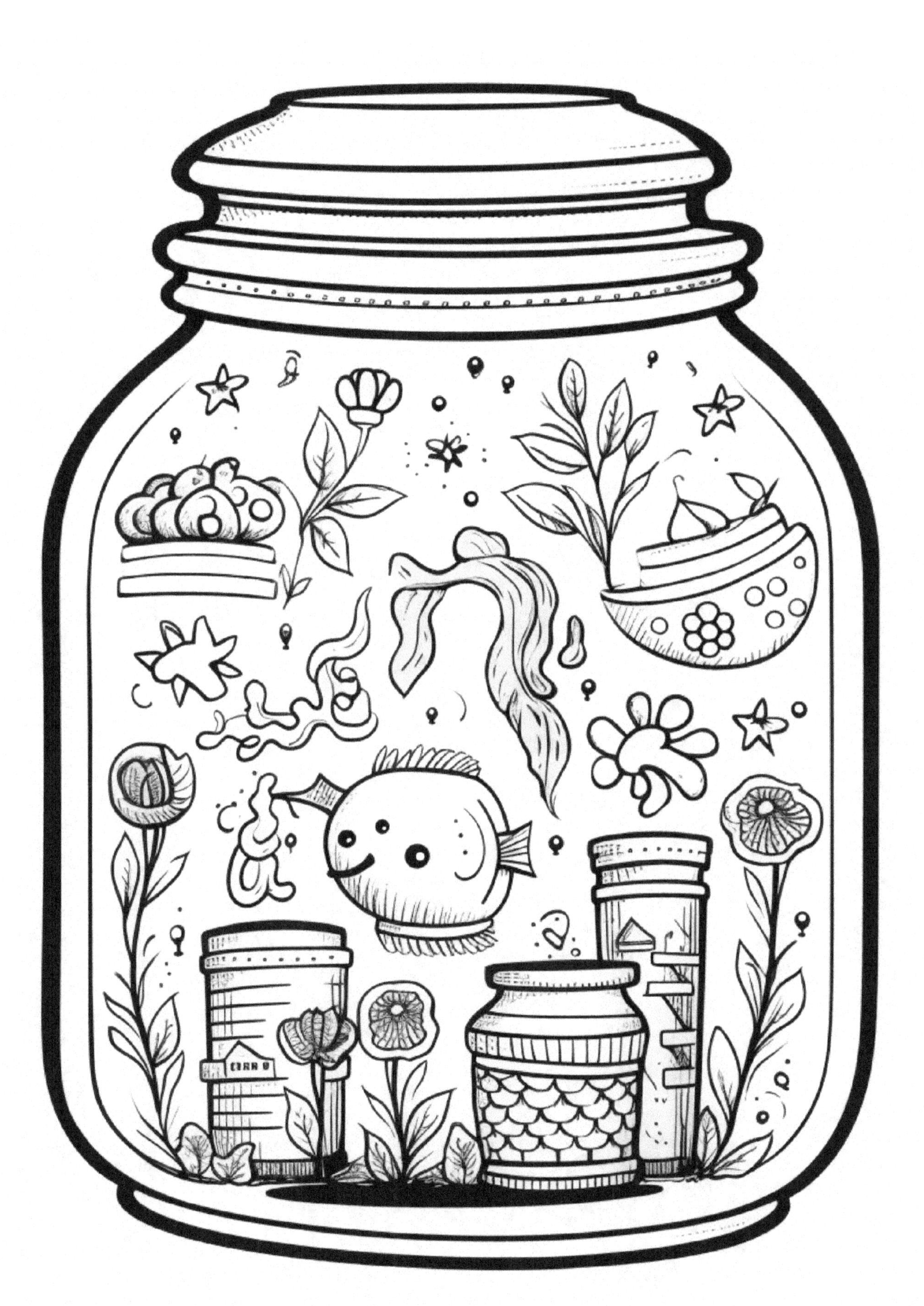

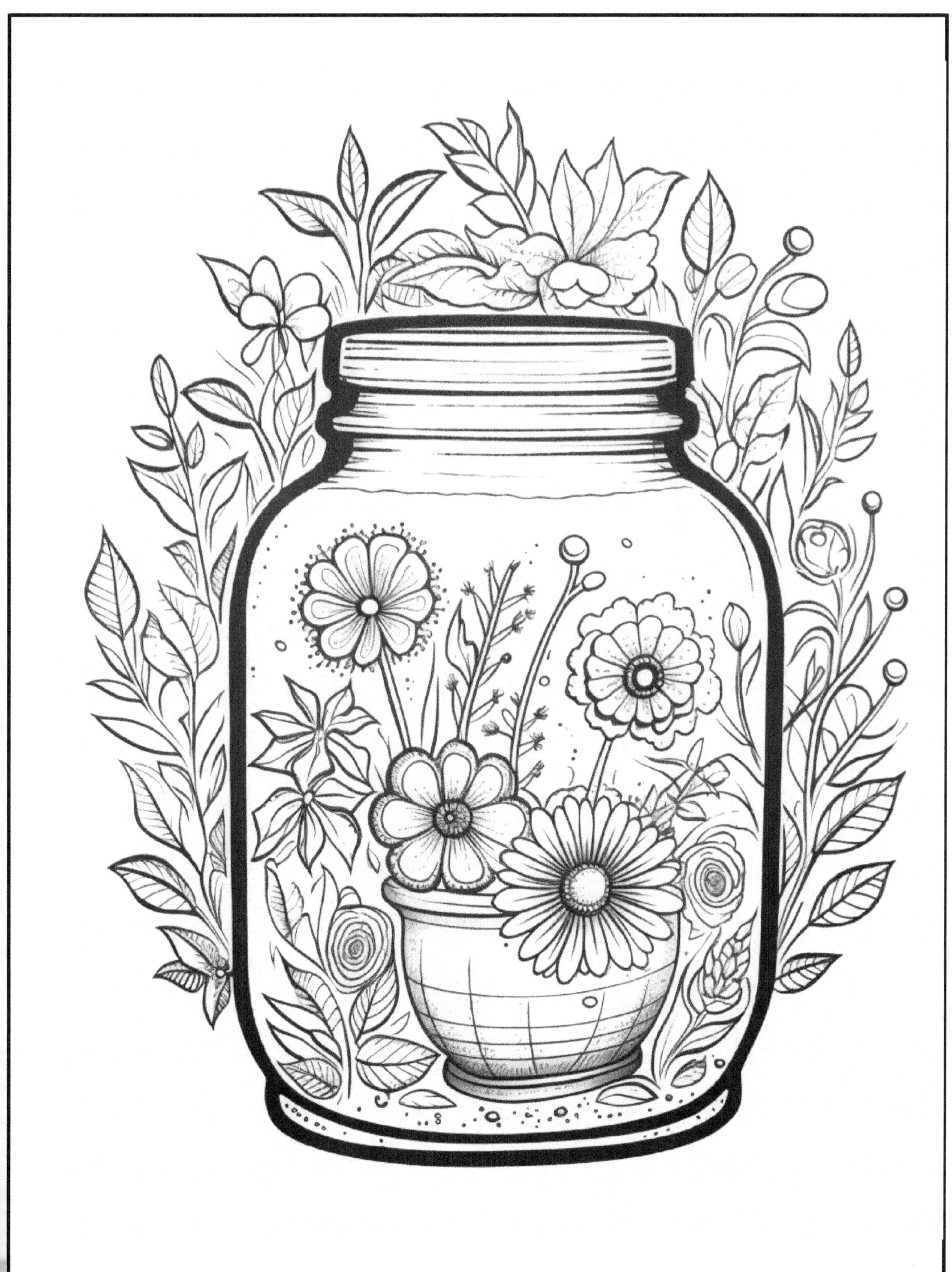

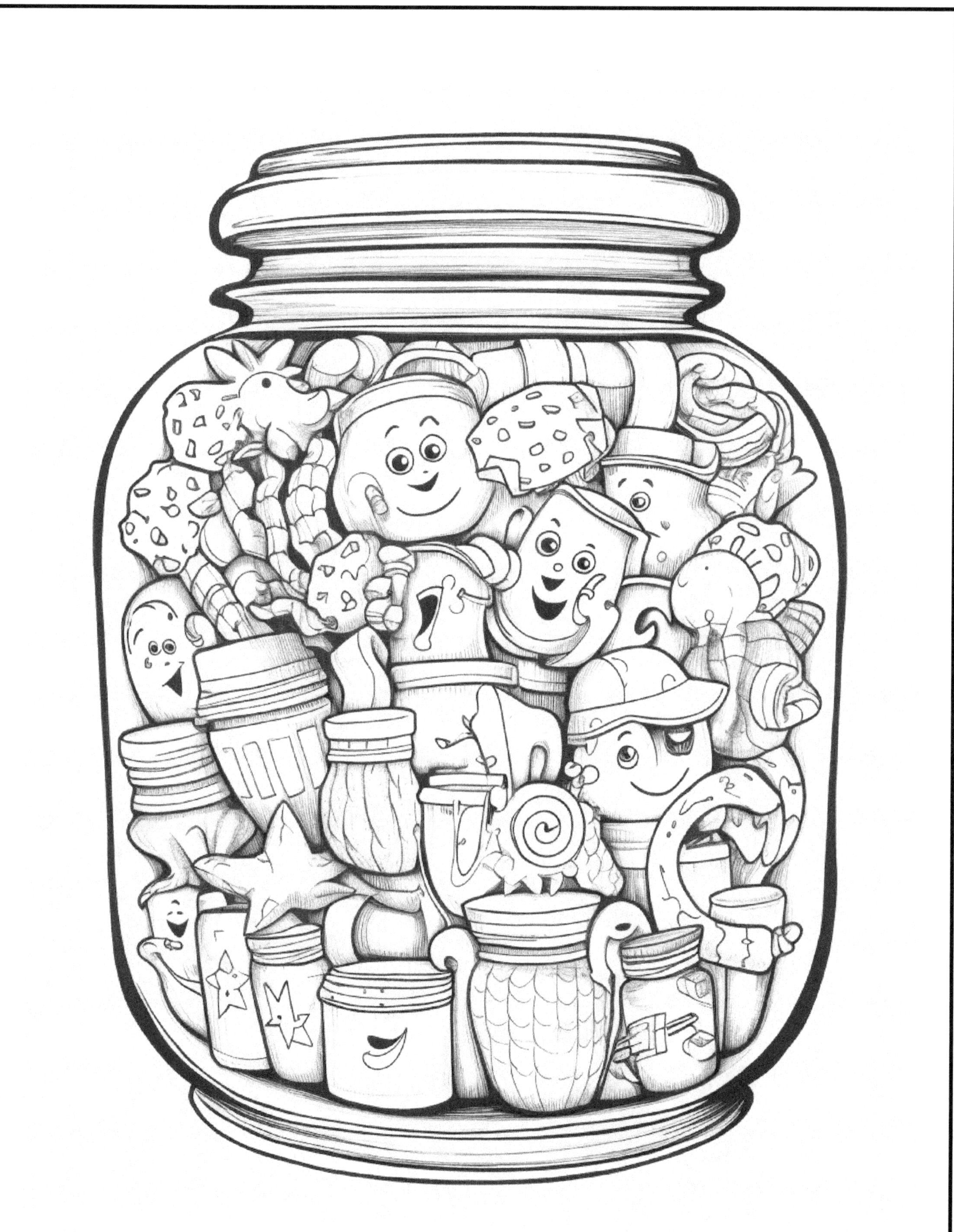

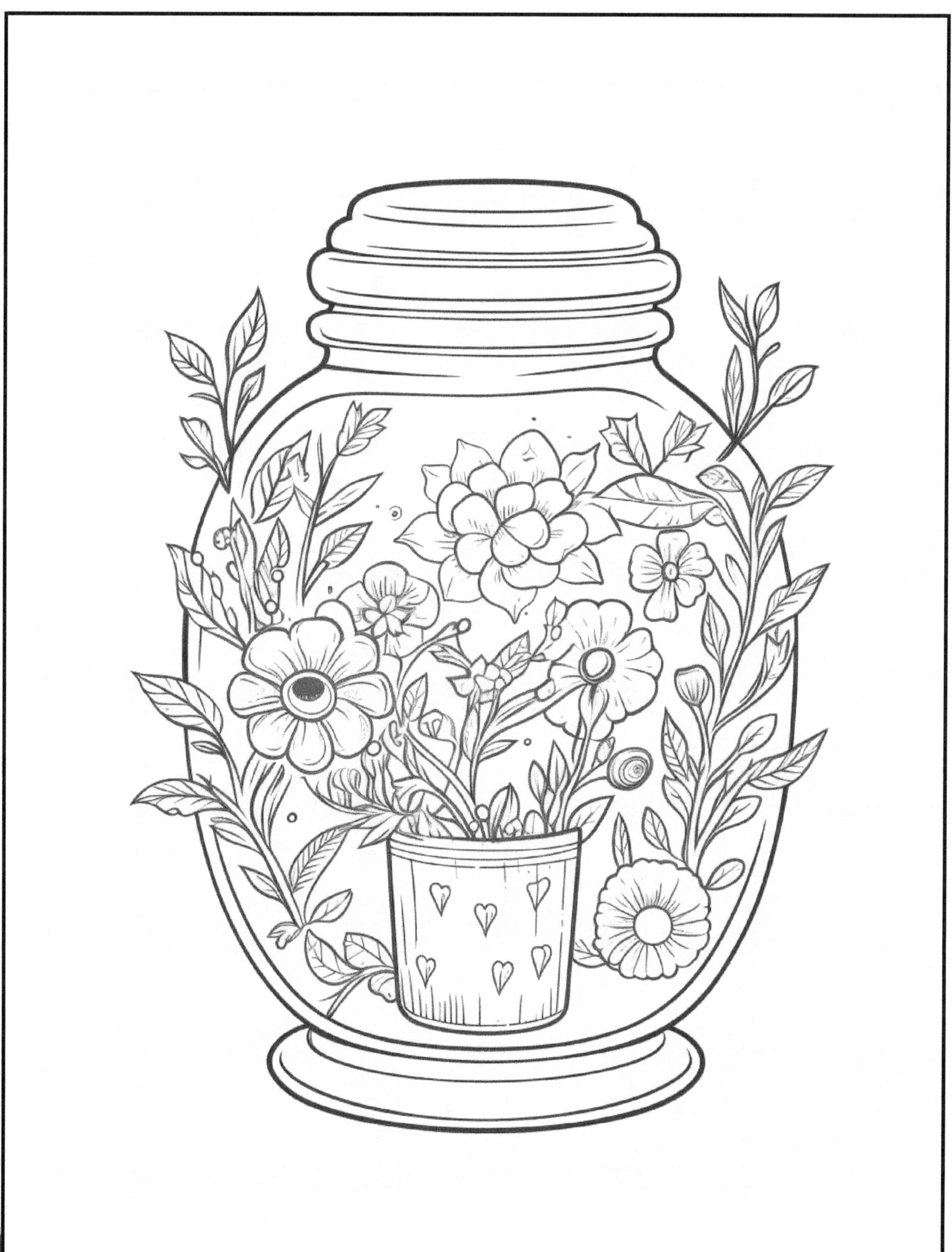

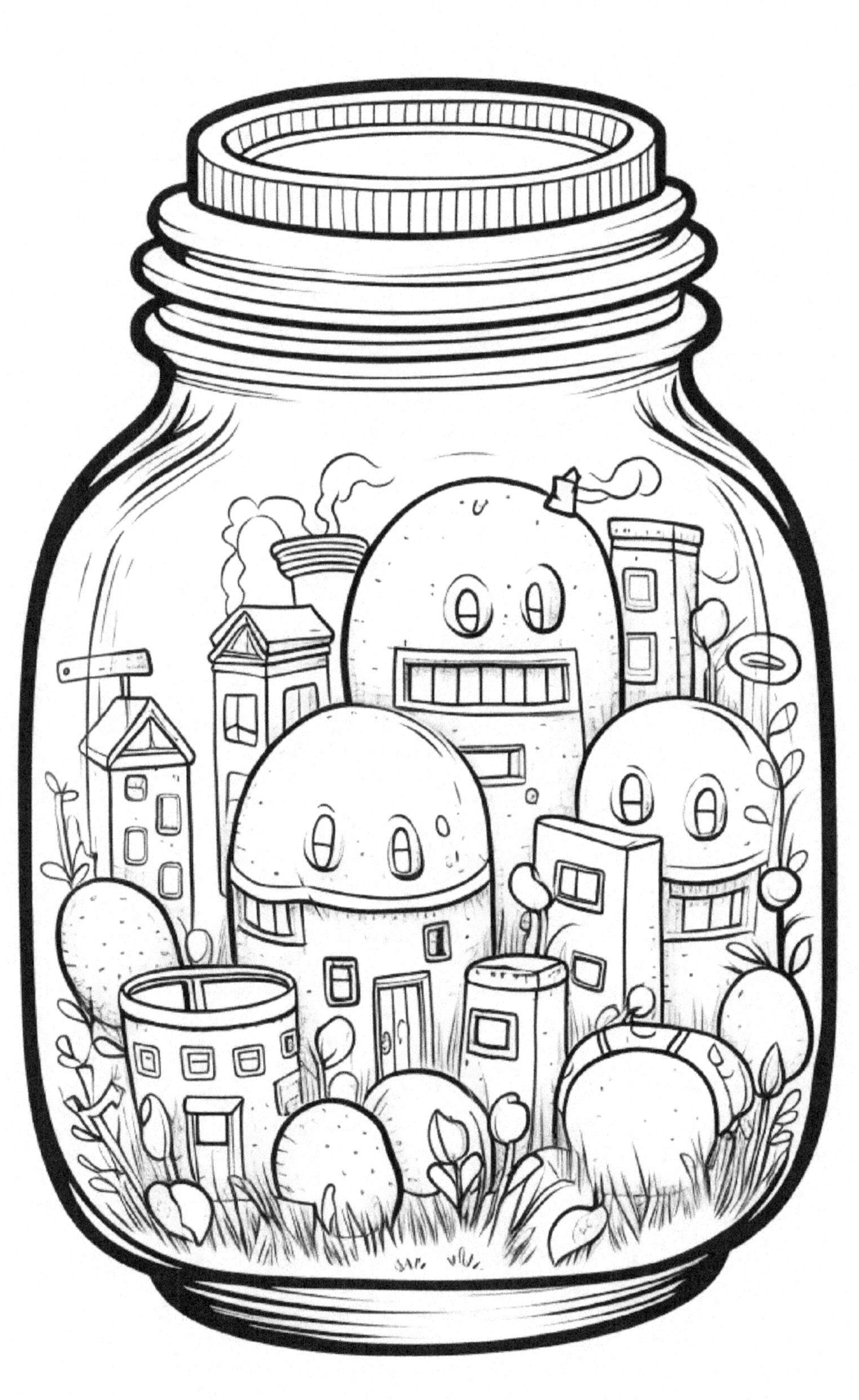

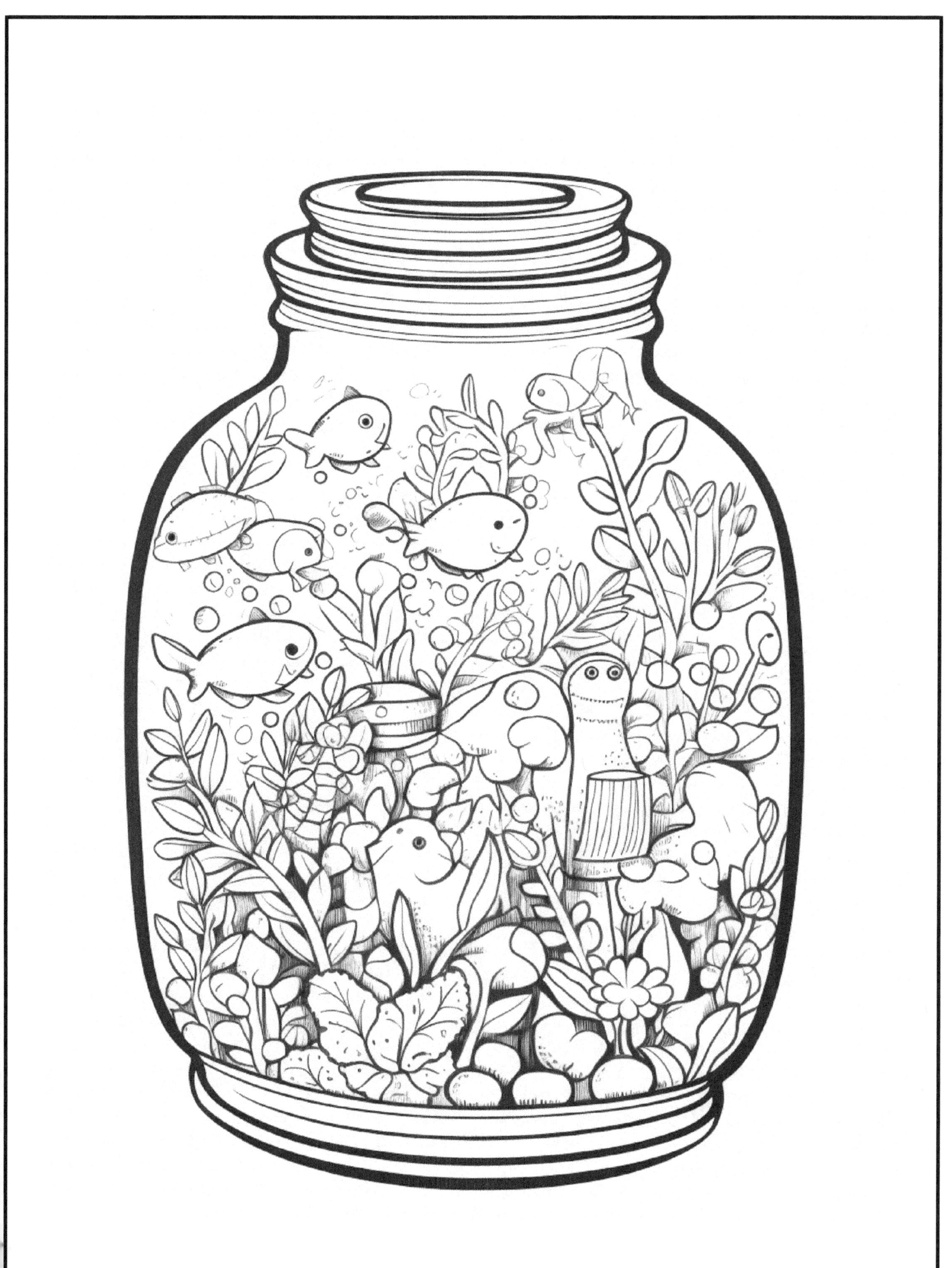

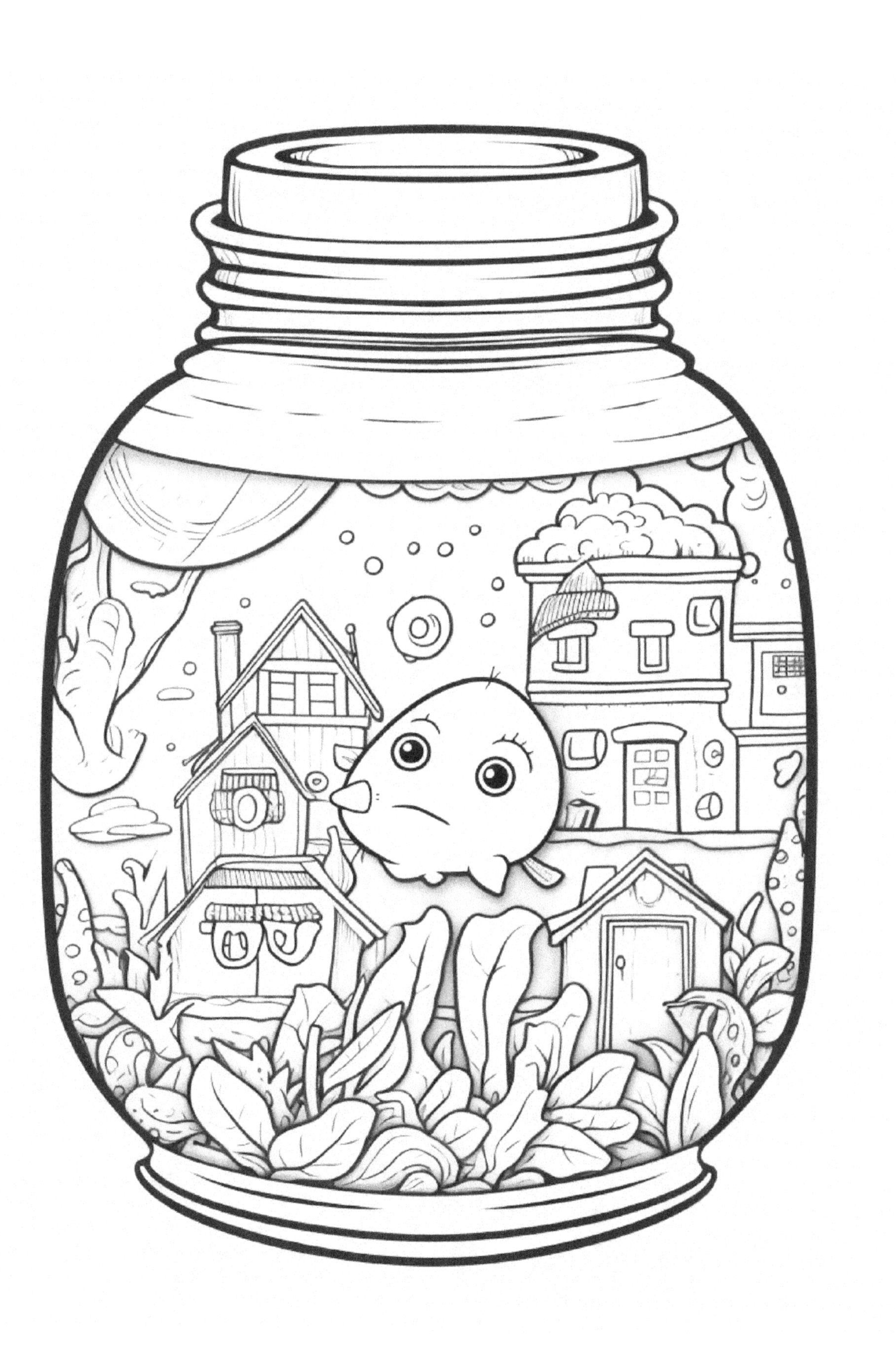

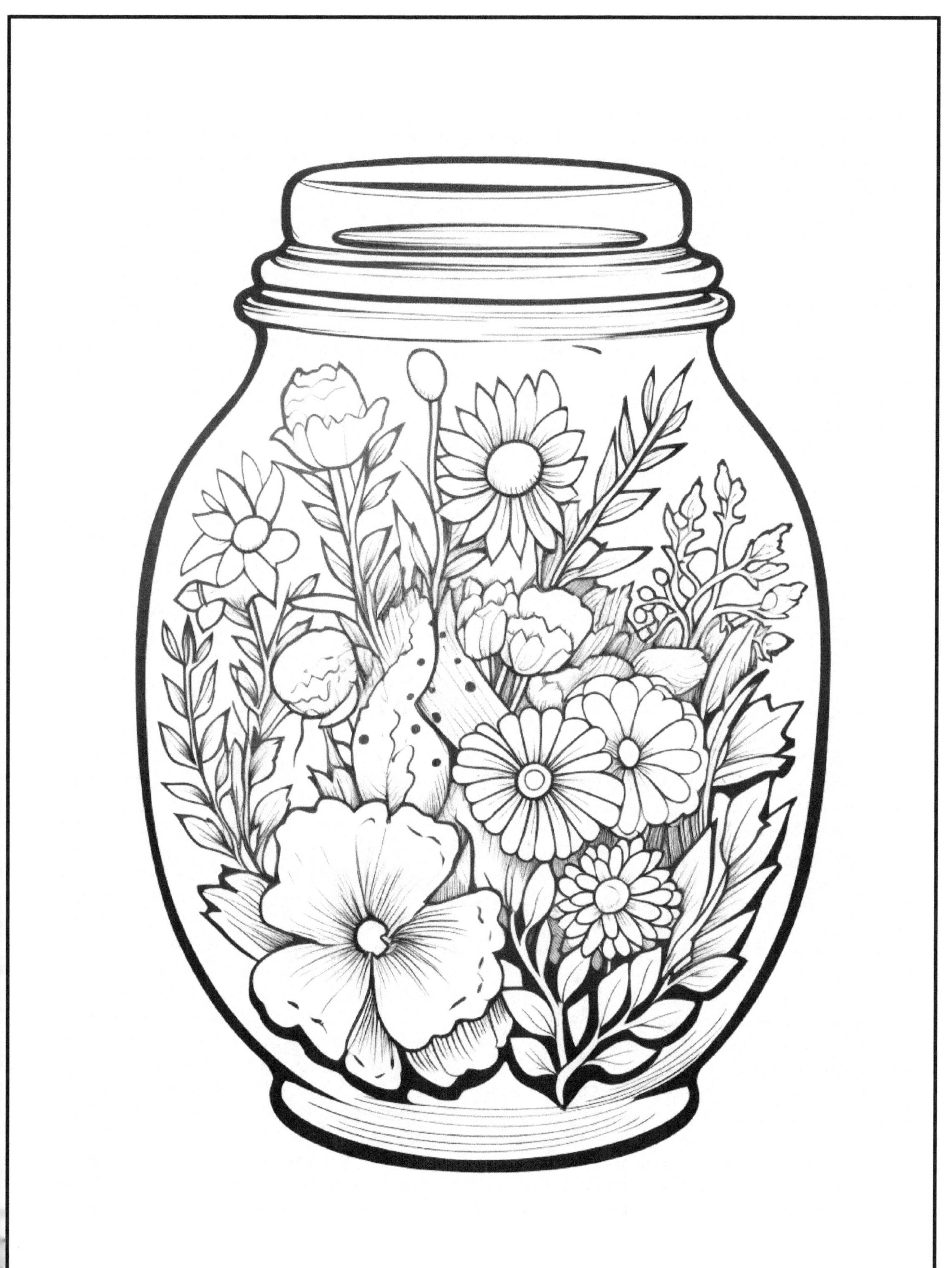

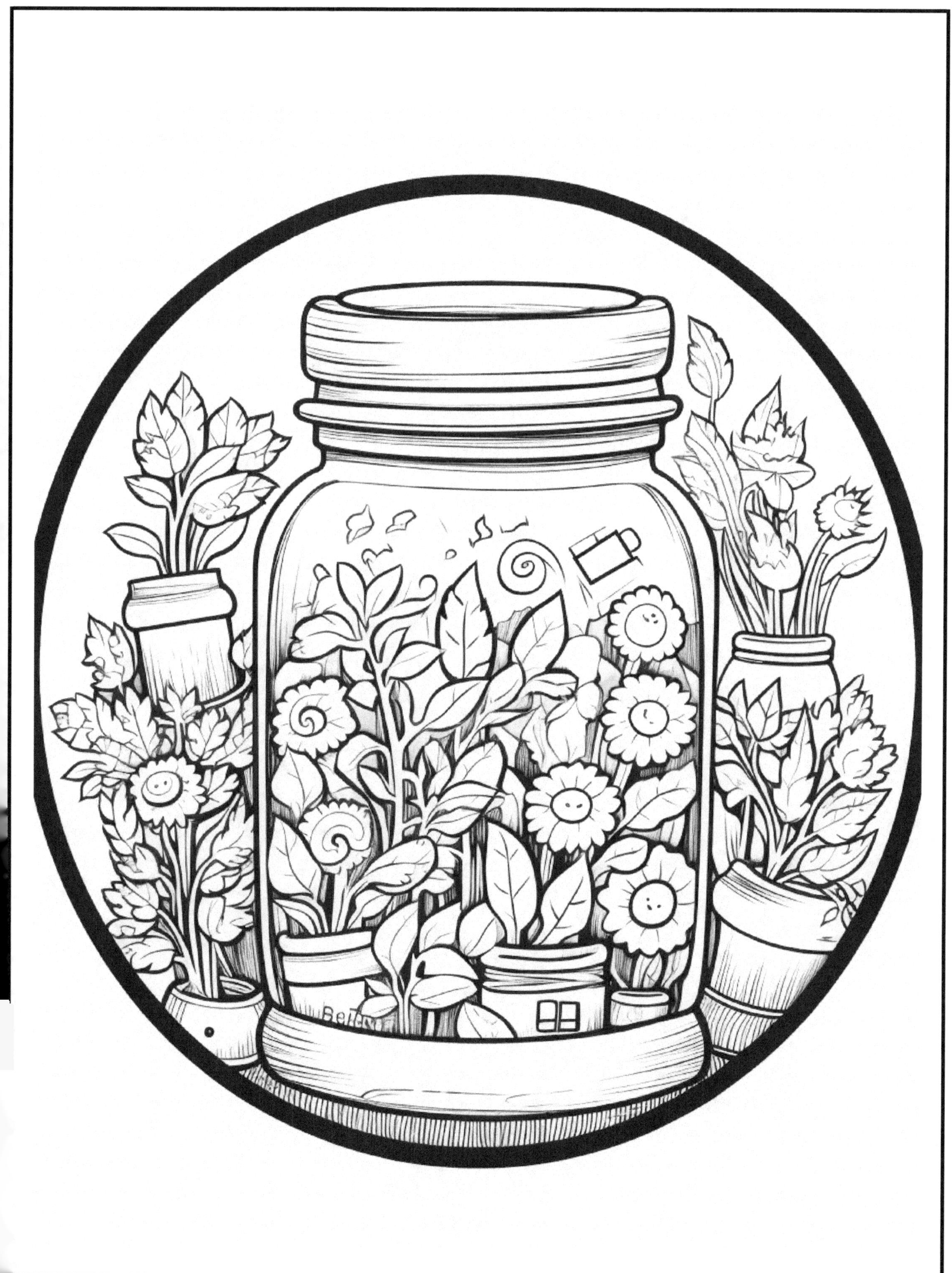

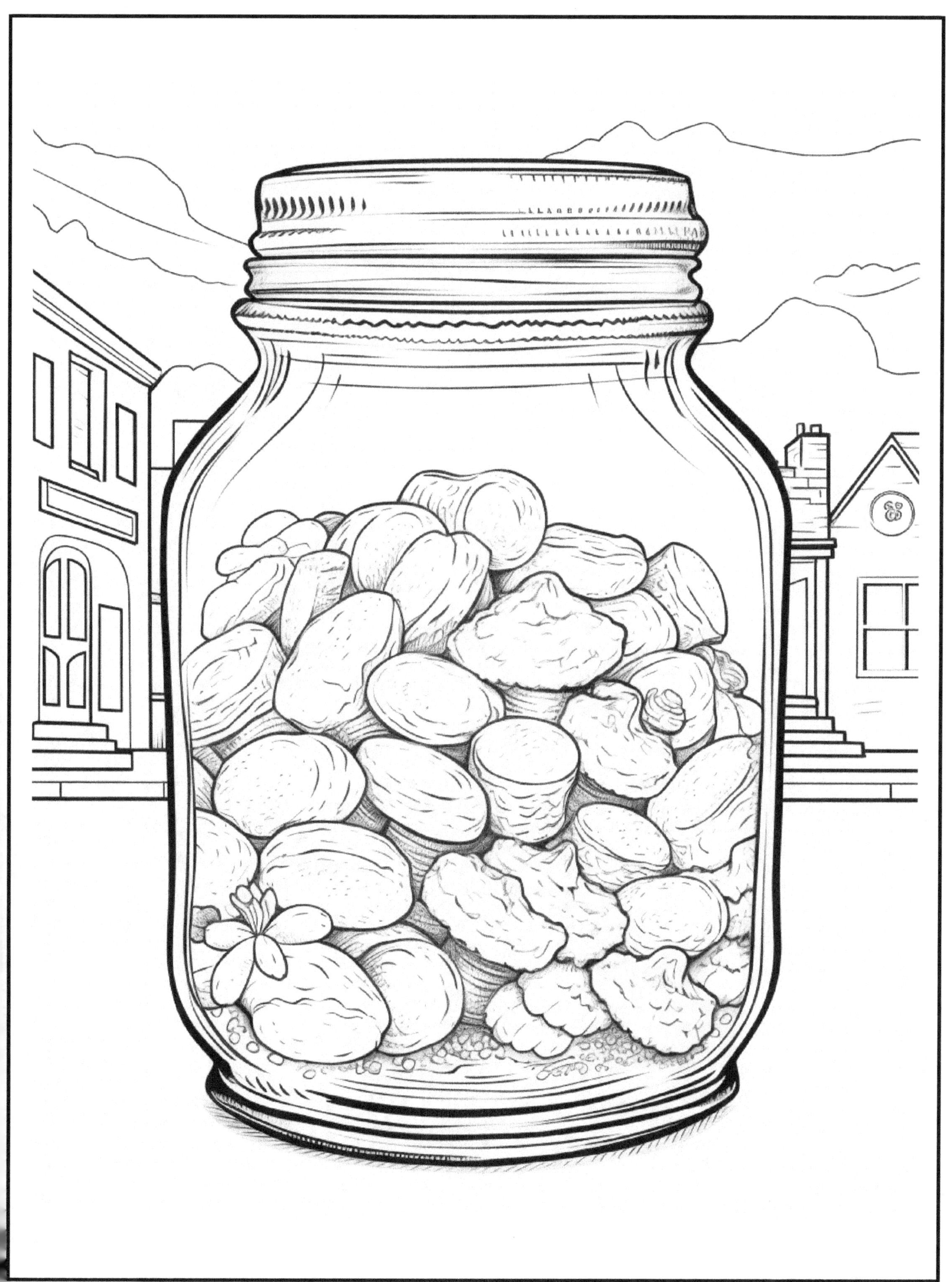

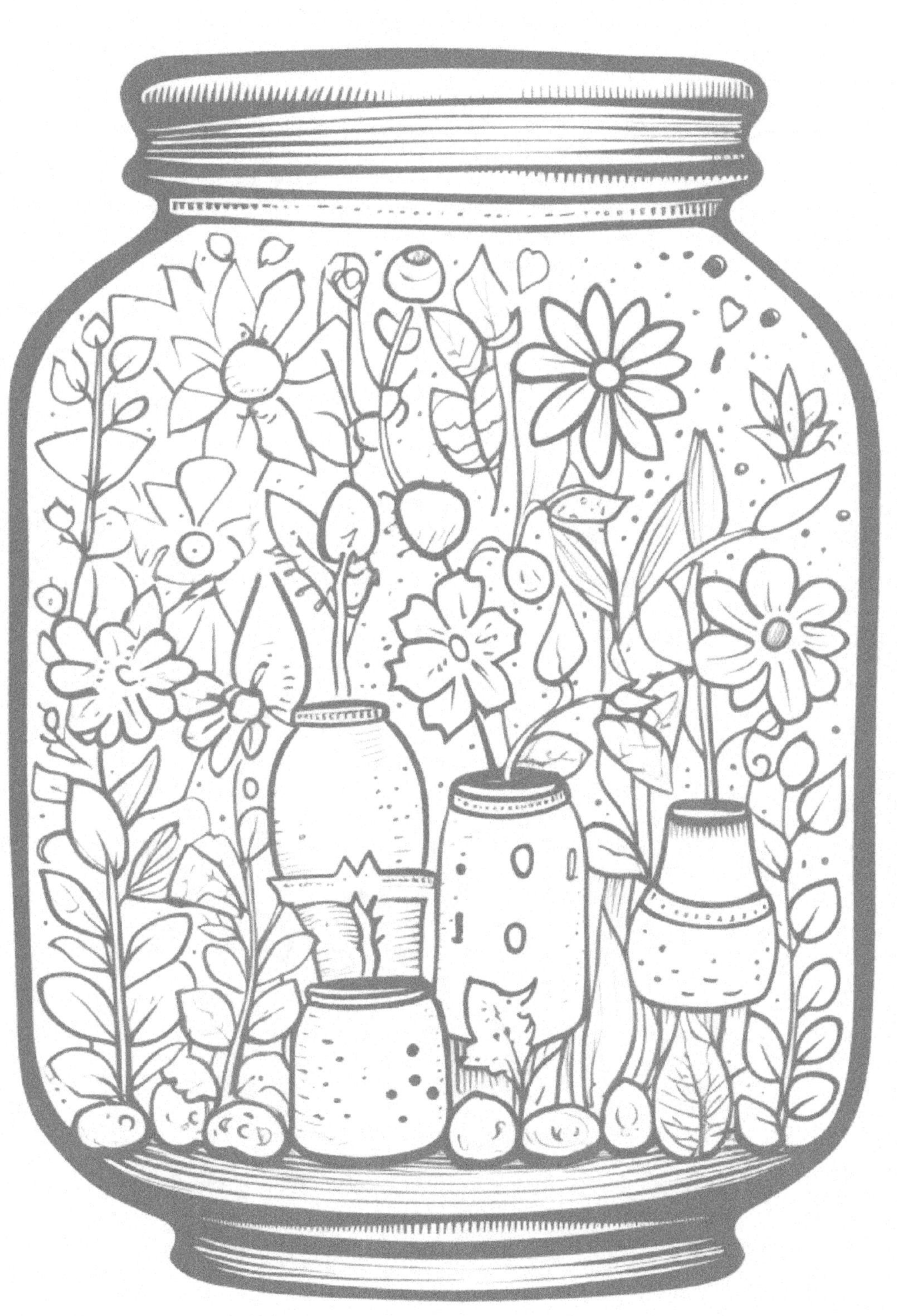

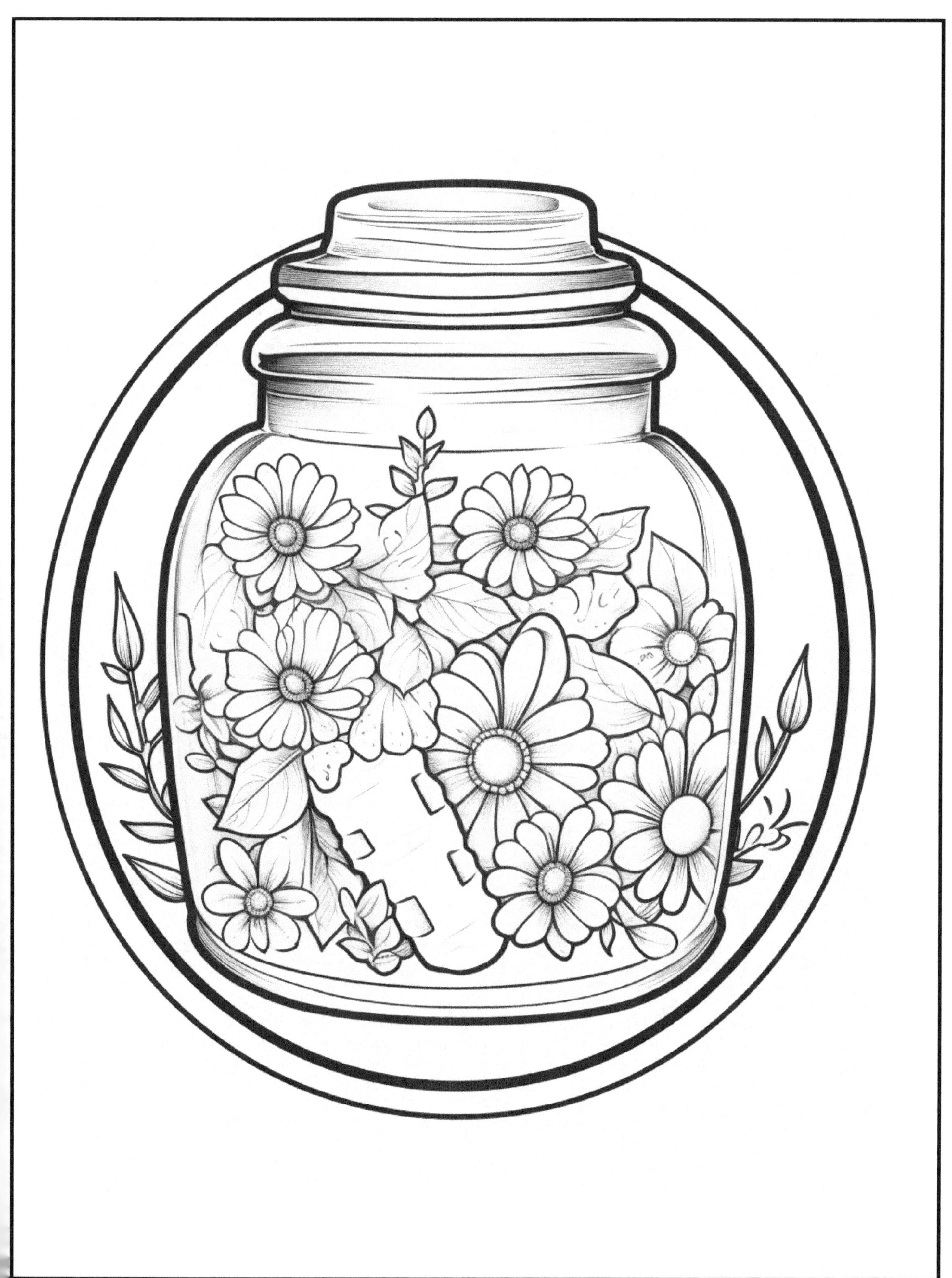

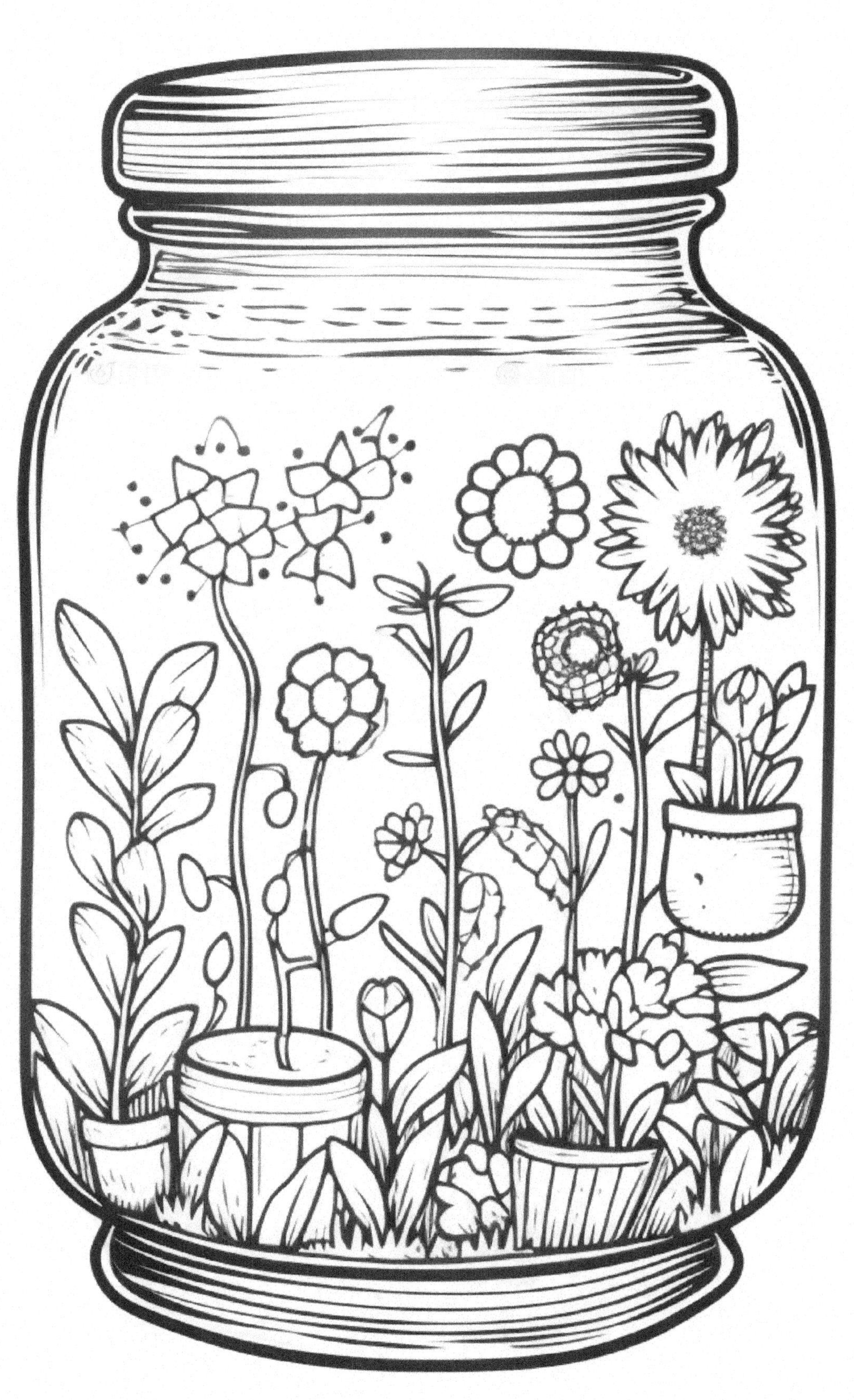

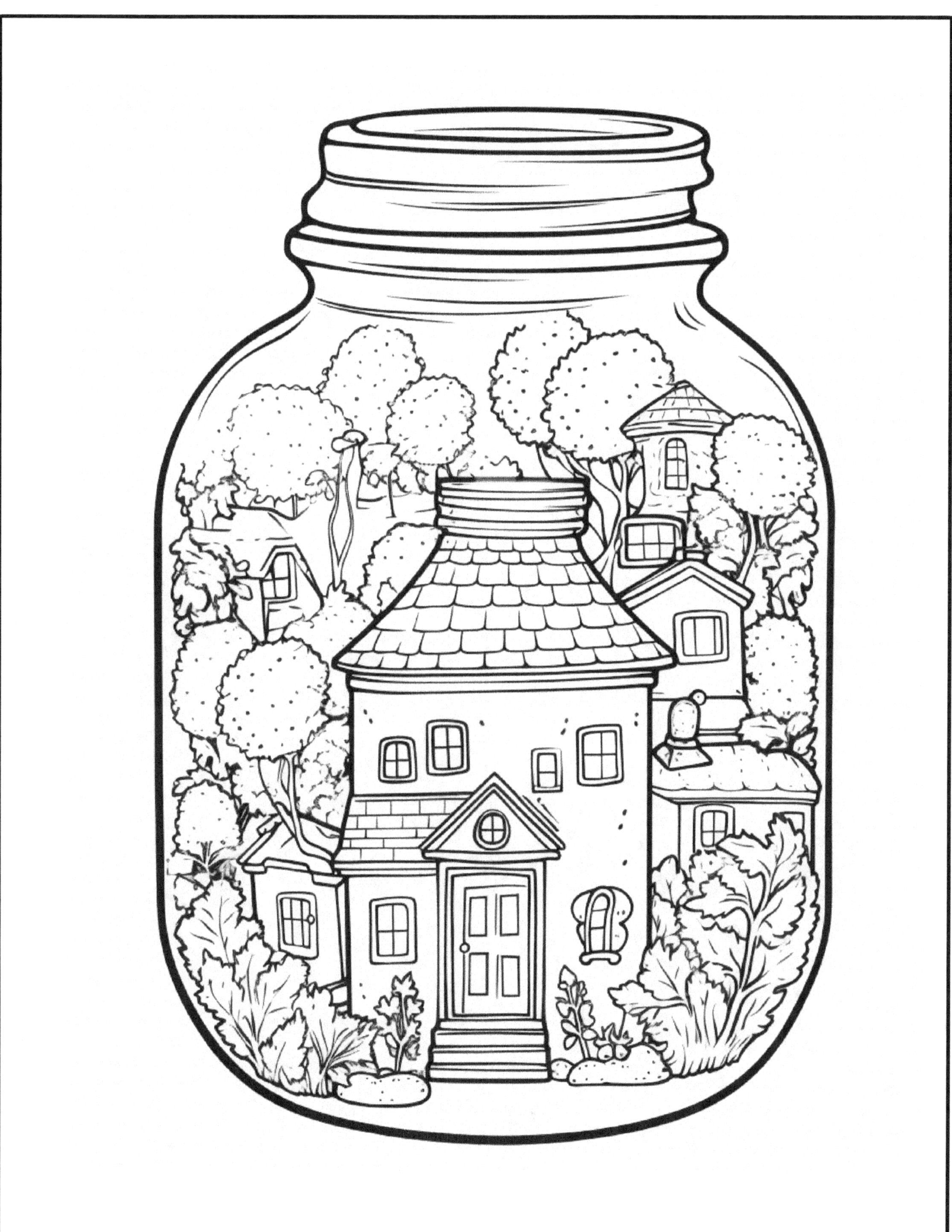

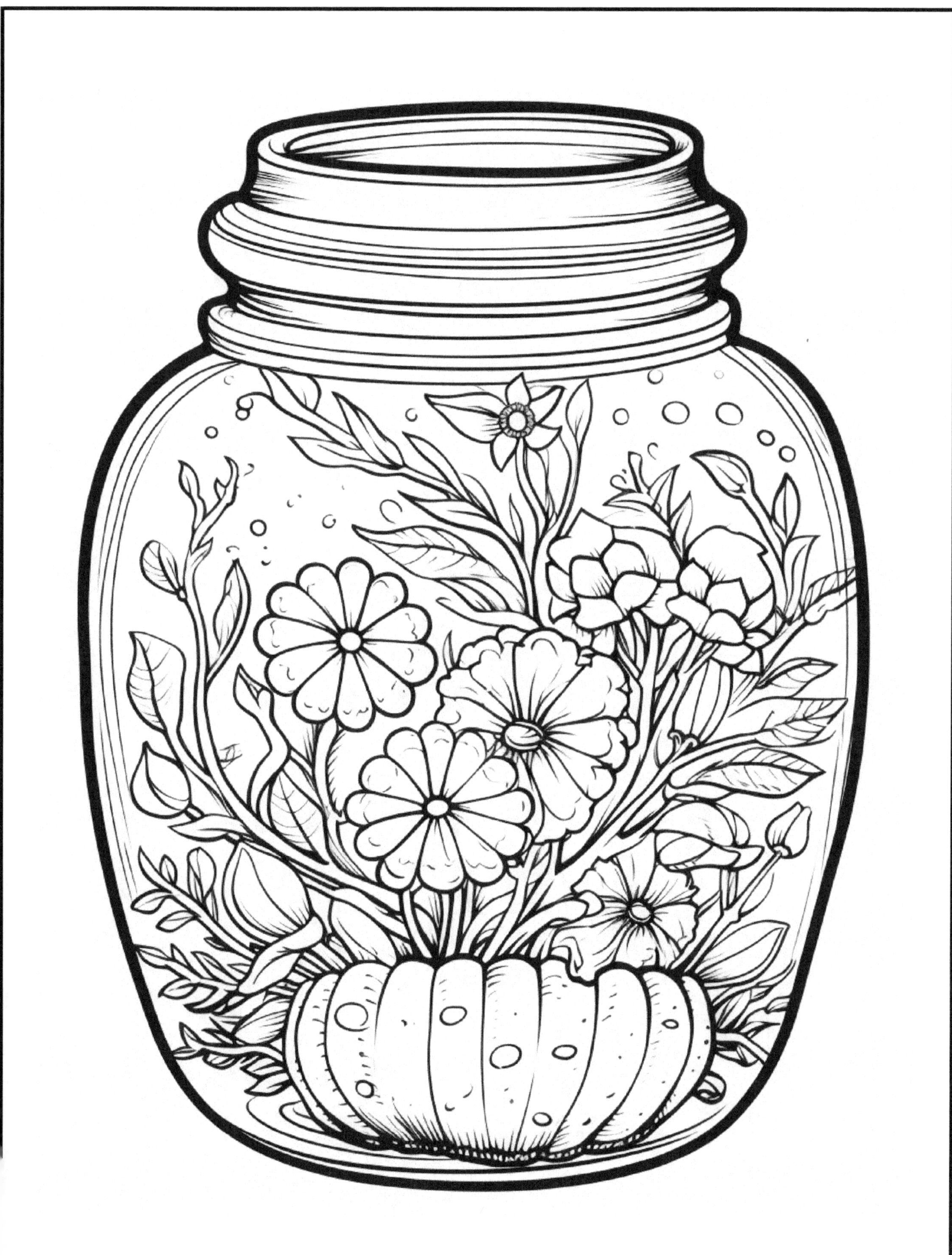

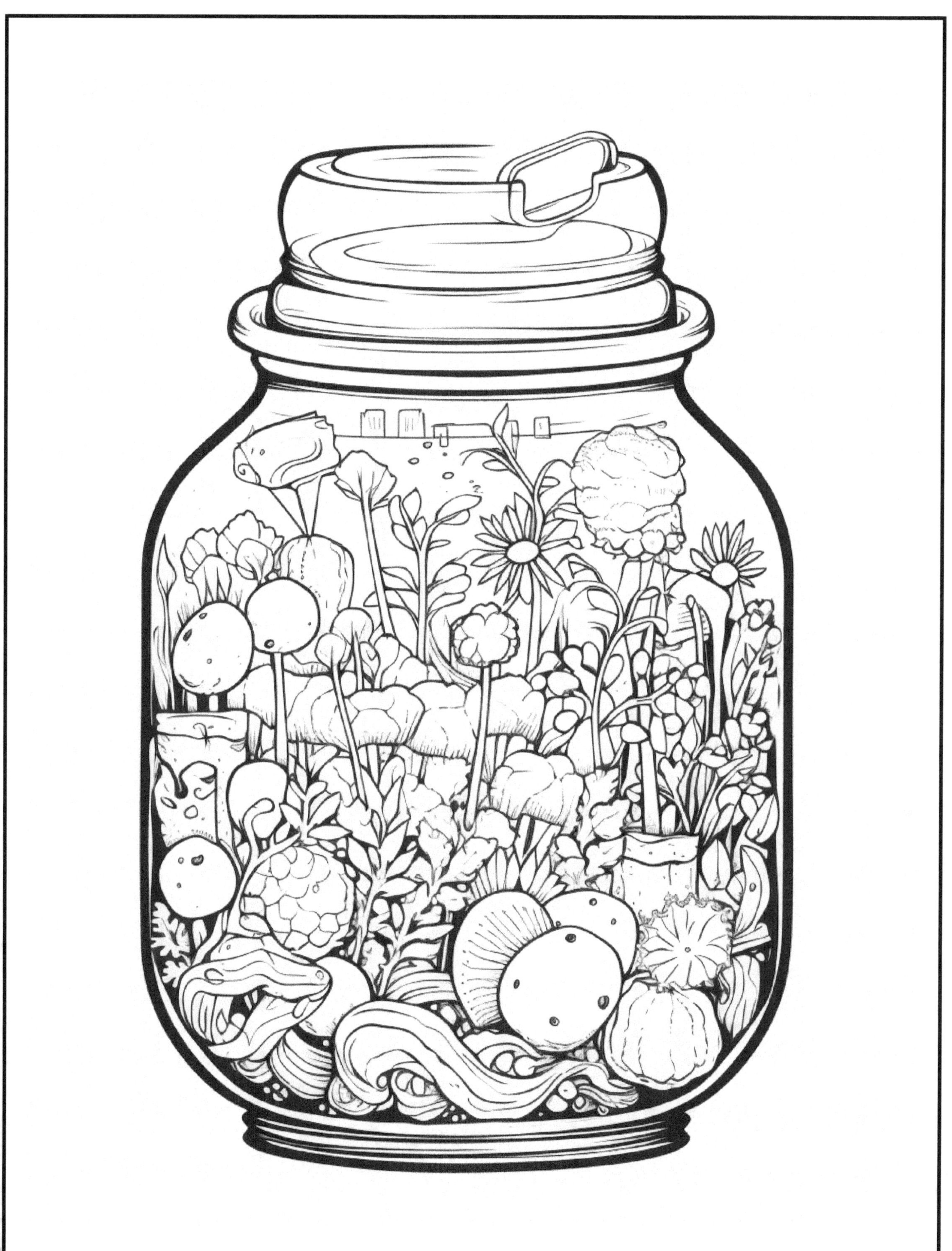

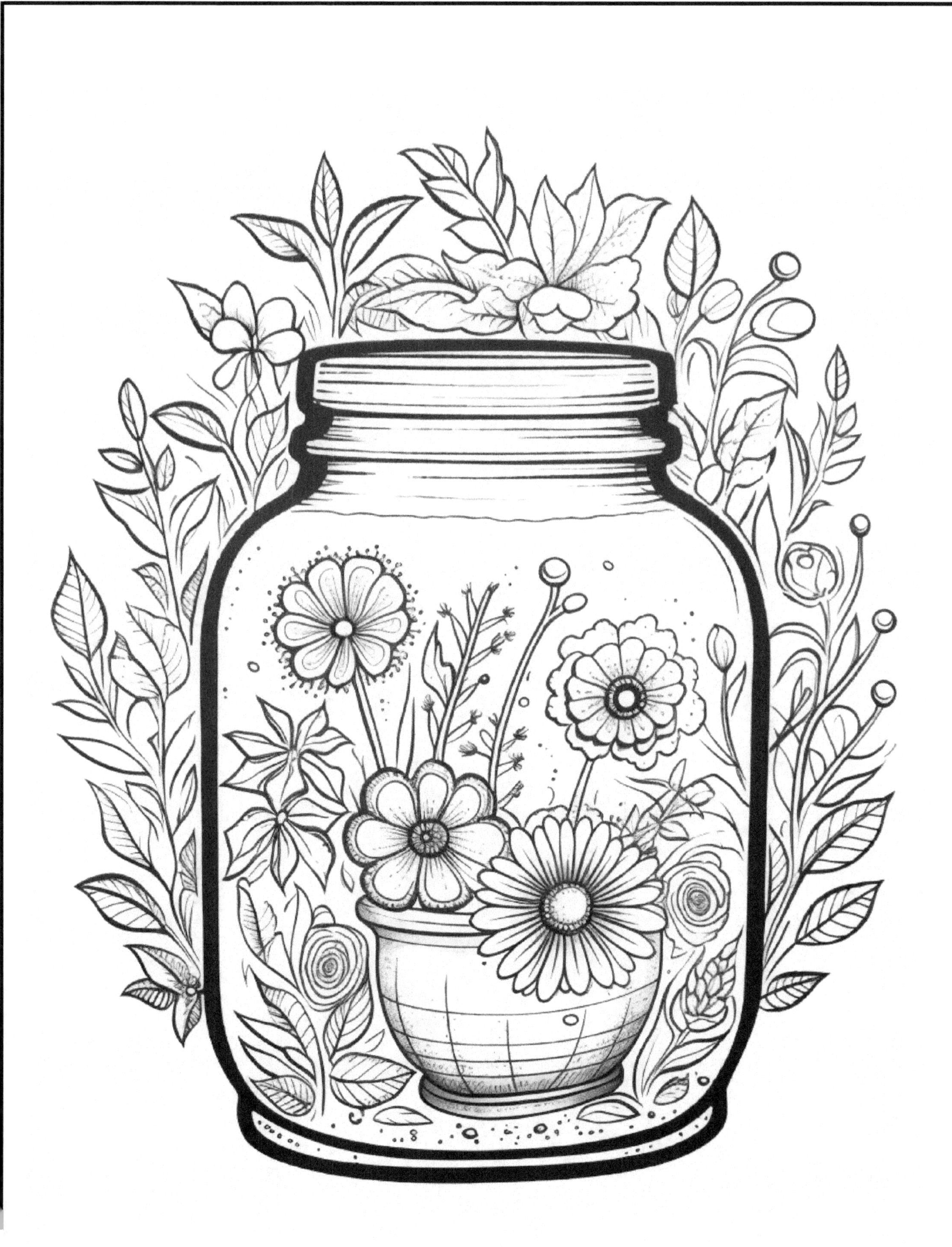

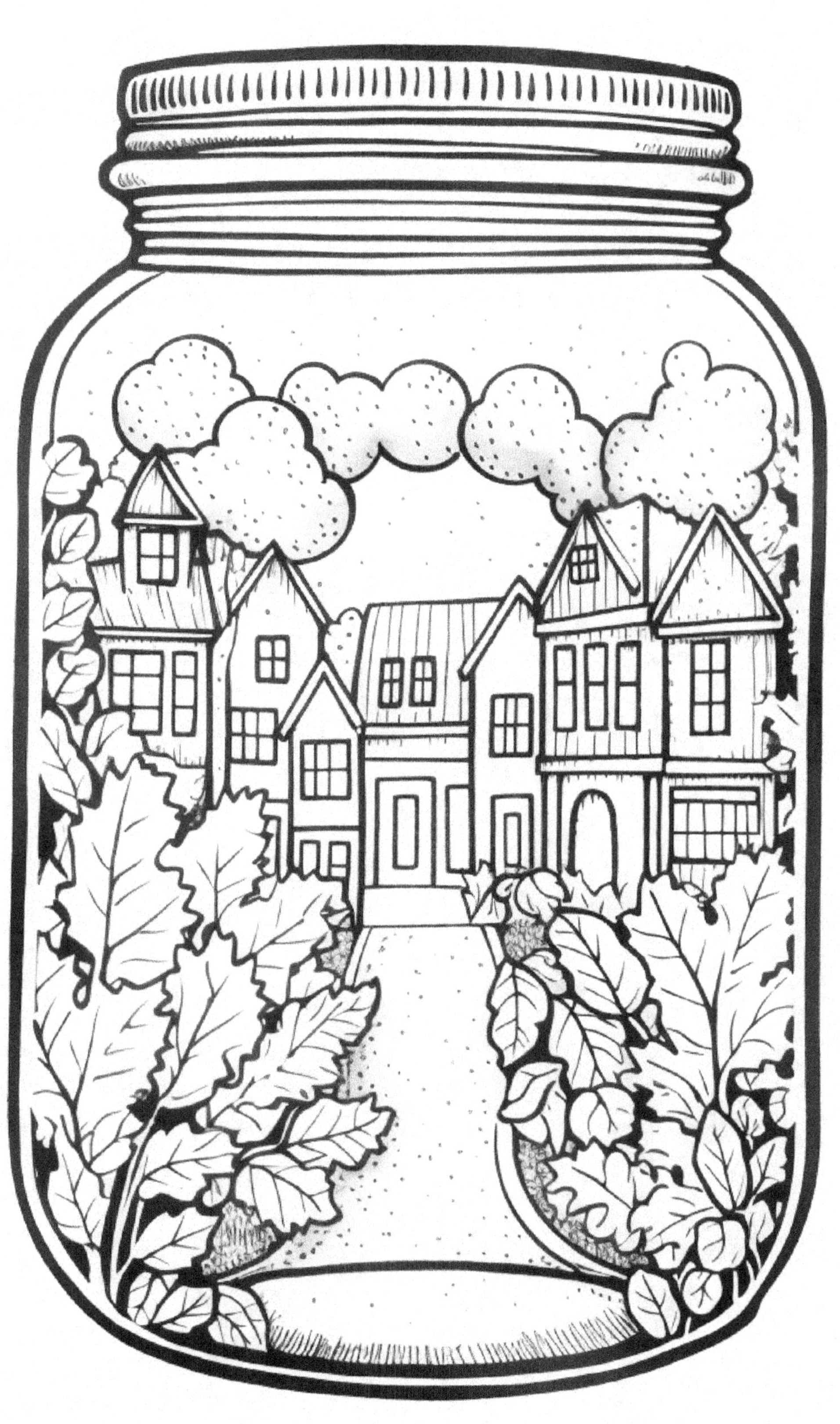

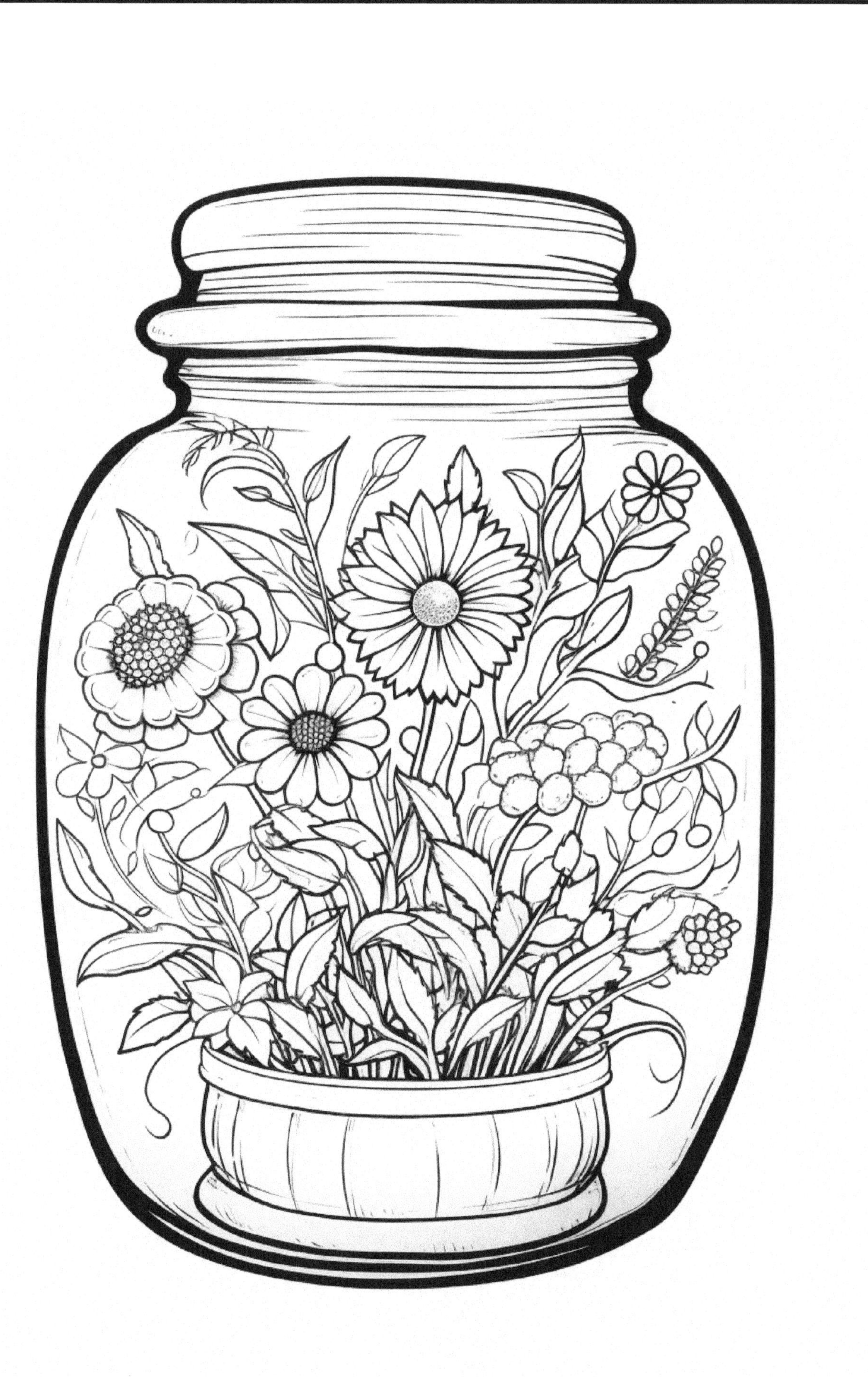

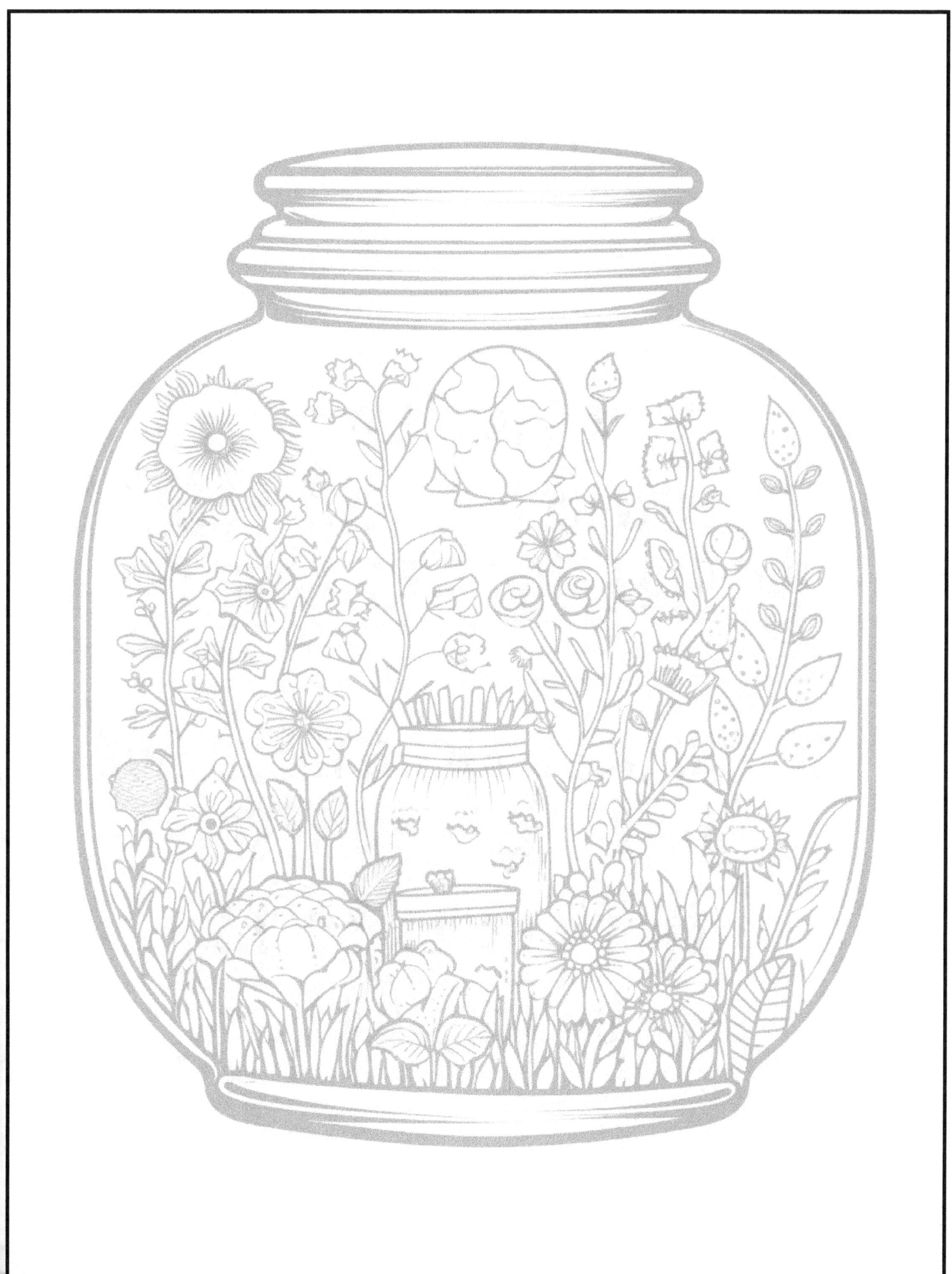

★THANKS★
FOR PURCHASING OUR BOOKS
WE HOPE YOU WILL LOVE IT.

IF YOU NEED ANY OTHER BOOK
THERE YOU CAN ALSO
CHECK OTHER BOOKS
IN OUR STORE

www.ingramcontent.com/pod-product-compliance
Lightning Source LLC
Chambersburg PA
CBHW081608270726
48661CB00021B/4066